⚽ PLAYING FOR THE KINGDOM⚽

A Devotional for Catholic Soccer Fanatics

by Charles T. Alexandra

Table of Contents

Note to Readers: *This devotional booklet is for private use and is intended to support athletes and their families in living out their faith through sport. All prayers and devotions are believed to be aligned with the teachings of the Catholic Church, though this booklet has not been formally approved by ecclesiastical authority.*

Dedication

To my wife, the ultimate soccer mom, whose unwavering support, patience, and love have carried our family through countless matches, muddy fields, and long road trips.

To my children, who continue to fill the Beautiful Game with wonder, joy, and purpose, keeping its magic alive in my heart.

And…to every player, every fan, every coach, and every referee - thank you for helping build this sacred corner of God's vineyard, where effort becomes prayer, and the game becomes grace.

Why I Wrote This Booklet

As a soccer player, coach, and father to two soccer-loving children, I've spent nearly fifty years immersed in the beautiful game. And over all those years, I've come to believe something deeply, **soccer is God's game**.

On its surface, it may just seem like any normal sport; eleven players, a ball, a goal. But those who've truly lived the game know better. Within those ninety minutes lie moments of grace, sacrifice, unity, discipline, heartbreak, resurrection, and joy. We see glimpses of the miraculous, goals that defy physics, comebacks that inspire the soul, courage that lifts the human spirit.

Soccer, also referred to: fútbol, football, calcio, futebol, fußball, voetbal, サッカ, футбол, and many more is not just a contest of physical strength or tactical skill. It is, for those who choose to see it, a sacred space, a field where we can practice our faith in the most real and embodied sense. Plus, it's global, bringing together different races, different cultures and different languages.

This booklet was born from that conviction.

- It's for every athlete who wants to invite Christ onto the pitch.
- For every parent who prays quietly from the sidelines.

For every coach who sees their role not just as building players, but forming mature adults.

Through these prayers, I hope to help faithful athletes and families bring their faith into the rhythm of the game, before the whistle blows, in the heart of competition, and long after the final score is forgotten. My goal is not to make sport religious in a superficial way, but to sanctify the game from the inside, to let it be another place where Christ is known, honored, and glorified.

Whether you're suiting up to play, driving to practice, coaching from the bench, or watching in the stands, may these prayers help you draw closer to God through the gift of the game.

In Christ,
Charles

General Prayers

Prayer for Courage and Discipline

Heavenly Father,

You are the source of all strength and order.
Before I step onto the field, I ask for Your grace:

Grant me courage, not only to face my opponents,
but to conquer fear, laziness, and self-doubt.

Give me discipline,
to train when I'm tired,
to hold my tongue when I'm tempted,
to play clean when I could cheat,
and to keep going when it would be easier to quit.

May I master myself before I try to master the game.
Let every sprint, every tackle, and every pass
be done with purpose, and offered to You.

Teach me to compete without pride,
to fight without hatred,
and to grow stronger in virtue through every trial.

Through the intercession of St. Sebastian,
and in the name of Jesus Christ, my King,
I pray.

Amen.

Prayer for Charity and Humility

Lord Jesus,

You humbled Yourself to serve and to save.
As I prepare to take the field,
root out the pride in my heart.

Let me not play to crush others,
but to honor You with my effort.

Help me treat every teammate with love,
every opponent with respect,
and every moment of the game as a chance
to grow in holiness.

When I succeed, may I not boast.
When I fail, may I not despair.

Remind me that this game—like my life—
is not about glory for myself,
but about becoming more like You.

May I play hard, speak kindly,
and reflect Your light,
even when no one is watching.

Through the example of Our Lady,
and the grace of Your Son,
guide me in humility and charity today.

Amen.

Prayer to Offer the Game to God

Father in Heaven,

I offer You this game,
every moment of it,
as a gift and a prayer.

I lay before You my sweat, my effort, my talent.
Let them become a small sacrifice of praise.

May my joy in playing reflect Your goodness.
May my struggles draw me closer to Your Cross.
May my teamwork show the unity You desire for us all.

Win or lose,
may I walk off the field today
having grown in faith, virtue, and love.

I unite this game to the perfect sacrifice of Your Son,
and ask that it help sanctify my soul
and bring You glory.

For the Sacred Heart of Jesus,
through the Immaculate Heart of Mary,
I offer You this day.

Amen.

Role-Based Prayers

Prayer for Goalkeepers

Lord God, my Defender,

You are the Watchman who never sleeps.
As I stand in goal, grant me Your vigilance.

Help me stay focused, alert, and calm even when others lose
theirs.

Let me not fear mistakes, but trust in Your strength working
through me.

Give me quick hands, steady feet, and a clear mind.
More than that, give me peace in pressure, and courage in every
moment.

Teach me to guard not only the net, but my heart—against
pride, anger, or despair.

May I protect my team with love, and lead with quiet
confidence.

St. Michael the Archangel,
who defends God's people,
pray for me.

Amen.

Prayer for Defenders

Heavenly Father,

You are my refuge and strength.
As a defender, You've called me to stand in the breach.

Give me a heart ready to sacrifice—
to cover for others, to block shots, to bear the weight.

Let me be a wall of unity and love for my teammates,
never seeking my own glory, but working for the good of all.

Make me bold in challenges, disciplined in positioning, and
quick to recover—not just on the field, but in life.

May I defend with honor, protect with wisdom, and help build
a team that trusts one another.

Through the prayers of St. Joseph,
Guardian of the Holy Family,
protect me and guide me.

Amen.

Prayer for Midfielders

Lord Jesus, Servant King,

You walked among us with humility and strength.
Help me as a midfielder to reflect You on the field.

Give me endurance to run when others stop, and courage to take
up the burden of both attack and defense.

Let me see the field with wisdom, moving not for my own sake,
but for the good of the team.

Help me hold the center not only in position, but in unity, spirit,
and service.

When the game becomes chaotic, make me a calming presence.
When others look for leadership, may they find someone who
plays with heart and holiness.

Come, Holy Spirit,
strengthen me to run the race and keep the faith.
Be with me now.

Amen.

Prayer for Forwards

Lord of all courage,

You call us to press forward and not be afraid.
As I step into the front lines of this game, give me boldness, not
for my glory, but Yours.

Help me make my runs with purpose, take my chances with calm,
and face every challenge without fear.

Let me be decisive, but not selfish; fast, but not reckless;
passionate, but never prideful.

Teach me to pursue higher goals, not just scoring points,
but building virtue, inspiring my teammates, and giving all I have
to You.

May I learn from every miss, and remain humble in every victory.

St. Peter, who leapt from the boat to reach Christ,
pray for me, that I may always move with faith.

Amen.

Prayer for Team Captains

Heavenly Father, Leader of all,

You raised up David to lead Your people,
and Christ served as Shepherd to the flock.
As I carry the responsibility of captain,
guide me to lead as You would.

Give me calm in chaos, wisdom in pressure, and strength to put others before myself.

Help me speak with encouragement, act with justice, and serve as a bridge between coaches and teammates.

When tempers flare or morale dips, let me be the one who lifts others up.

Teach me to lead not just with voice or effort, but with character and faith.

Through the intercession of St. Joan of Arc, courageous and faithful in battle, be my guide.

Amen.

Prayer for Coaches

Lord of Wisdom and Truth,

You taught with parables, patience, and love.
As a coach, let me imitate You in all I do.

Help me see beyond wins and losses, and focus on the growth of each player; in skill, in discipline, and in spirit.

May I guide justly, correct gently, and lead with conviction and compassion.

Give me the grace to mentor, not just manage; to inspire, not just instruct.

Let every drill, talk, and decision help shape my players into better athletes and better people.

Grant me, Lord, a heart like Solomon's, not seeking riches or power, but wisdom to discern what is right.

Let Your wisdom guide my choices,
that I may serve You and others well today.

Amen.

Prayer for Referees

God of Justice and Peace,

You are the righteous Judge, slow to anger and rich in mercy.
As I take on the role of referee, give me the grace to be fair, calm,
and courageous.

Help me see clearly, act decisively, and remain unshaken by
pressure or complaint.

May I protect the game, honor its spirit, and treat all players with
dignity.

When I am questioned or criticized, let me respond with truth and
patience.

Remind me that my authority is for service, and that my judgment
must reflect integrity and justice.

St. John the Baptist,
fearless voice of truth in the wilderness,
pray for me.

Amen.

Prayers for Parents

Prayer for Soccer Moms

Blessed Mother Mary,

You watched your Son grow,
cheered Him in His hidden years,
and stood by Him through every joy and sorrow.

As a soccer mom, I bring You my heart,
full of hopes, worries, and endless car rides.

Help me live this vocation with grace.
May I encourage without pressuring,
support without controlling,
and love my child no matter the scoreboard.

Sanctify the small things; the packed snacks, folded jerseys, and
sideline prayers. Let my presence reflect Your maternal strength
and peace.

Teach me to surrender outcomes, and to entrust my child's heart
to the Sacred Heart of Jesus.

Be with me in the stands, in the car, and in the quiet moments
after the game.

Amen.

Prayer for Soccer Dads

St. Joseph, Guardian of the Redeemer,

You raised Jesus with quiet strength and steady love.
Help me, as a soccer dad, to follow your example.

Let me be a father who is present, cheering with joy, correcting with love, and always pointing toward what matters most.

Teach me to support my child in victory and defeat, to model hard work and humility, and to never let sport become an idol.

Bless my time on the sidelines, and in every conversation afterward; that my words may build up, and my actions reflect Your fatherly wisdom.

May this game become not just a contest,
but a classroom of virtue,
where my child learns to play, to love, and to trust in God.

Amen.

Prayer for Both Parents

Heavenly Father,

Thank You for the gift of our child
and the opportunity to walk this journey together.

As soccer parents, help us stay united -
in love, in support, and in prayer.

Remind us that wins and losses pass quickly,
but the virtues of faith, perseverance, and humility endure.

Let us be a team, encouraging our child, building each other up,
and keeping Christ at the center.

When we get caught up in performance, bring us back to peace.
When tensions rise, grant us grace.

We entrust our child, and this whole journey,
to Your plan and providence.

May our home always be filled with joy,
patience, and Your presence.

Amen.

Prayers for Fans

Prayer for Holy Enthusiasm as a Fan

Focus: *Joyful support, good sportsmanship, and keeping Christ at the center.*

Lord Jesus,

Thank You for the joy of the game and the gift of being part of this community of sport.

As I watch and cheer today, keep my heart full of joy, not judgment.

Let my words be uplifting, my spirit generous, and my eyes open to the beauty You've placed in every player, on both teams.

Help me to remember that this game, like all good things, is Yours.

Let my enthusiasm reflect Your goodness, not only when things go our way, but even in moments of disappointment.

May I never forget that people matter more than points, and that love is the highest goal of all.

Amen.

Prayer for Unity & Peace Among Supporters

Focus: *Avoiding division, rooting for peace, and uniting through love of the game.*

Lord God,

In a world so often divided, thank You for the gift of sport that brings people together.

Let today's game be a sign of unity, not rivalry.

Help all fans - of every team - to cheer with passion but never with hate,
to support with energy but never with prideful arrogance.

Keep violence and harshness far from our hearts.

Let us see one another not as enemies, but as brothers and sisters who love the beautiful game.

May the joy of the match lead us to the joy of communion with You.

Amen.

Prayer of Trust in Victory or Defeat

Focus: *Acknowledging God's will in the outcome of the game.*

Heavenly Father,
You are Lord over every moment, on the field and beyond it.

As I cheer today, I lift my heart to You.

Let my joy not depend on the score,
but on the goodness You show in all things.

If we win, may I celebrate with humility.

If we lose, may I accept it with grace.

In every outcome, Your will be done.

Teach me to see Your hand even in disappointment,
and to praise You for the lessons hidden in defeat.

Help me encourage those around me, players, coaches, and fellow fans,
with words that build up, not tear down.

Let my love for the game never exceed my love for You.

You are the true victory, the prize that lasts forever.

Amen.

9-Day Tournament Novena

to

Christ the King

(Best if followed leading up to the tournament)

Day 1 – Confidence in God's Strength

Opening Prayers

Hail Mary, full of grace, the Lord is with thee.
Blessed art thou among women, and blessed is the fruit of thy womb, Jesus.
Holy Mary, Mother of God, pray for us sinners, now and at the hour of our death. Amen.

Our Father, who art in heaven, hallowed be Thy name;
Thy kingdom come, Thy will be done on earth as it is in heaven.
Give us this day our daily bread, and forgive us our trespasses,
as we forgive those who trespass against us.
And lead us not into temptation, but deliver us from evil. Amen.

Glory be to the Father, and to the Son, and to the Holy Spirit,
as it was in the beginning, is now, and ever shall be, world without end.
Amen.

Scripture Verse

"I can do all things in Him who strengthens me." — Philippians 4:13

Reflection

In this tournament, pressure will come. The scoreboard may rise and fall. But Christ never changes.
He is the same yesterday, today, and forever, the rock beneath our feet when the ground seems to shake. Our performance might fluctuate, but His love does not. His presence is not earned by goals scored or mistakes avoided.

On the field, we may face opponents faster or stronger than we are. We may feel the weight of expectations; our own, our team's, or others watching. But God is not measuring our worth by the final score. He sees our hearts, our efforts, our courage to keep going.

True strength doesn't come from adrenaline or muscle, it comes from grace. From knowing that even when we are weak, He is strong in us.

Today, I will not play for applause or comparison. I will play for Him. Every sprint, every pass, every moment of focus and fatigue will be my offering. Because when I give it all to Christ, the game becomes more than a competition, it becomes a prayer.

Petition

Jesus, my King,
give me confidence not in my own ability,
but in Your presence within me.
Let me step onto the field with peace and trust,
knowing that whatever happens, I play for Your glory.

Closing Prayer

Lord Jesus Christ, King of Heaven and Earth,
I give You this day, this game, this tournament.
Strengthen me in body and soul.
Let every pass, every run, every breath be for You.
Whether I win or lose, let me become more like You—
faithful, courageous, and full of love. Amen.

Day 2 – Humility in Victory and Defeat

Opening Prayers

Hail Mary, full of grace, the Lord is with thee.
Blessed art thou among women, and blessed is the fruit of thy womb, Jesus.
Holy Mary, Mother of God, pray for us sinners, now and at the hour of our death. Amen.

Our Father, who art in heaven, hallowed be Thy name;
Thy kingdom come, Thy will be done on earth as it is in heaven.
Give us this day our daily bread, and forgive us our trespasses,
as we forgive those who trespass against us.
And lead us not into temptation, but deliver us from evil. Amen.

Glory be to the Father, and to the Son, and to the Holy Spirit,
as it was in the beginning, is now, and ever shall be, world without end.
Amen.

Scripture Verse

"Whoever exalts himself will be humbled, and whoever humbles himself will be exalted."
— Matthew 23:12

Reflection

Whether we win or lose today, let us remember that we are nothing without Christ. He is our source, our sustainer, and our ultimate end. Every ability I have, the strength to run, the skill to pass, the vision to see the play - is a gift. And every outcome, whether a thrilling victory or a heartbreaking loss, is permitted by His providence for our good.

Victory is a gift to be received with gratitude, not a trophy for our egos. If we win, we will not boast, for the glory belongs to God alone. We will honor Him by lifting others, not ourselves. And if we lose, we will not despair. Defeat is a hidden teacher, forming in us the virtues of patience, resilience, and detachment from worldly praise.

What matters most is not the scoreboard, but the state of our souls. We are not the center of this game or this life—Christ is. Our worth does not come from fans, stats, or trophies. It comes from being a beloved son or daughter of the King, claimed by His Cross and called to His Kingdom. That truth holds firm no matter what happens today.

Petition

Jesus, humble of heart,
teach me to rejoice without boasting,
and to accept loss without bitterness.
Keep me small in my own eyes,
and great in my love for You and others.

Closing Prayer

Lord Jesus, true King and Servant of all,
guard my heart from pride.
Let my confidence rest in You alone.
In moments of success, keep me grateful.
In moments of failure, keep me faithful.
Use this game to form in me the heart of a true disciple—
gentle, humble, and full of grace. Amen.

Day 3 – Perseverance Through Fatigue

Opening Prayers

Hail Mary, full of grace, the Lord is with thee.
Blessed art thou among women, and blessed is the fruit of thy womb, Jesus.
Holy Mary, Mother of God, pray for us sinners, now and at the hour of our death. Amen.

Our Father, who art in heaven, hallowed be Thy name;
Thy kingdom come, Thy will be done on earth as it is in heaven.
Give us this day our daily bread, and forgive us our trespasses,
as we forgive those who trespass against us.
And lead us not into temptation, but deliver us from evil. Amen.

Glory be to the Father, and to the Son, and to the Holy Spirit,
as it was in the beginning, is now, and ever shall be, world without end.
Amen.

Scripture Verse

"Let us run with perseverance the race that is set before us, keeping our eyes fixed on Jesus."
— Hebrews 12:1–2

Reflection

Tournaments push the body and the will. As the minutes wear on, fatigue sets in, muscles ache, lungs burn, and the mind begins to doubt. The temptation is to coast, to give in, to preserve energy instead of giving it all. But perseverance isn't born in ease; it's born in adversity. It is in the final stretch, when strength fades, that true character emerges.

The saints teach us that suffering, offered in love, becomes sanctifying. Christ Himself did not turn back when His body failed. He fell, but rose again, carrying His Cross all the way to Calvary. He teaches us that perseverance isn't about being the strongest or fastest. It's about continuing, step by step, in love and obedience, even when it hurts.

Today, every sprint, every recovery run, every extra ounce of effort is our offering. We may not feel strong, but we will give everything we have, not for glory or medals, but as a prayer. Our perseverance can become a form of worship. We will carry our crosses through the final whistle, trusting that Jesus walks with us and that grace meets us where our strength ends.

Petition

Jesus, my Strength,
when I am tired, lift me.
When I want to quit, remind me of Your Cross.
Help me to fight on—not just for a win,
but for the growth of my soul and the glory of Your name.

Closing Prayer

Lord Jesus Christ,
You endured every pain for the joy set before You.
Help me to push through today's challenges with faith.
Let my perseverance be a prayer,
my effort a gift,
and my heart a place where You reign.
I play for You. Amen.

Day 4 – Love for Teammates and Opponents

Opening Prayers

Hail Mary, full of grace, the Lord is with thee.
Blessed art thou among women, and blessed is the fruit of thy womb, Jesus.
Holy Mary, Mother of God, pray for us sinners, now and at the hour of our death. Amen.

Our Father, who art in heaven, hallowed be Thy name;
Thy kingdom come, Thy will be done on earth as it is in heaven.
Give us this day our daily bread, and forgive us our trespasses,
as we forgive those who trespass against us.
And lead us not into temptation, but deliver us from evil. Amen.

Glory be to the Father, and to the Son, and to the Holy Spirit,
as it was in the beginning, is now, and ever shall be, world without end.
Amen.

Scripture Verse

"Love one another as I have loved you."
— John 15:12

Reflection

The game brings out emotion - joy in a beautiful goal, frustration when a pass is missed, even anger when the game feels unfair. But Jesus calls us to love, not just when it's easy, but especially when it's hard. This kind of love isn't soft or passive. It's strong and disciplined. It means choosing to respect the dignity of others, even in the heat of competition.

Today, we want to look beyond the jerseys and positions. Our teammates are not just athletes, they are brothers and sisters, each with their own struggles and dreams. And our opponents? They are not enemies. They are children of God, created with purpose, beloved by the same Savior who died for all of us.

The world teaches us to compete with pride and aggression. Christ teaches us to compete with love and honor. We want to play with fire in our hearts but never allow that fire to consume kindness. We will give our all on the field, but not at the cost of our souls. Winning means nothing if we lose our integrity. Today, we will compete fiercely and love fiercely, too.

Petition

Jesus, Divine Love,
soften my heart on the field today.
Help me speak kindly, forgive quickly,
and play with a spirit of brotherhood and respect.
May my actions reveal Your love, even in the heat of the match.

Closing Prayer

Lord Jesus,
You laid down Your life for us.
Help me to play with selflessness and love.
Let my words build up, not tear down.
Let my spirit lift others, not crush them.
Make me a teammate others can trust,
and an opponent others can respect. Amen.

Day 5 – Peace Under Pressure

Opening Prayers

Hail Mary, full of grace, the Lord is with thee.
Blessed art thou among women, and blessed is the fruit of thy womb, Jesus.
Holy Mary, Mother of God, pray for us sinners, now and at the hour of our death. Amen.

Our Father, who art in heaven, hallowed be Thy name;
Thy kingdom come, Thy will be done on earth as it is in heaven.
Give us this day our daily bread, and forgive us our trespasses,
as we forgive those who trespass against us.
And lead us not into temptation, but deliver us from evil. Amen.

Glory be to the Father, and to the Son, and to the Holy Spirit,
as it was in the beginning, is now, and ever shall be, world without end.
Amen.

Scripture Verse

"Peace I leave with you; My peace I give to you.
Not as the world gives do I give to you.
Let not your hearts be troubled, neither let them be afraid."
— John 14:27

Reflection

Pressure is part of the game. The stakes rise, and so do the nerves - penalty kicks with everything on the line, final minutes in a tied match, the noise of the crowd, the expectations of teammates, the fear of letting someone down. These moments can feel overwhelming, even paralyzing. But the voice of Christ cuts through the chaos: *"Peace I leave with you; My peace I give to you."*

This peace isn't the absence of stress or the guarantee of success, it's the unshakable presence of Jesus in the middle of it all. The world says we need to prove ourselves. That we have to win to be worthy. But Christ says, *"You are already mine."* We don't have to carry the weight alone. We only need to trust Him and be present, to play each moment with faith, not fear.

With Jesus, we can be calm even in the storm. Our value doesn't come from performance but from His love. Whether we take the final shot or sit on the bench, He is with us. Today, we choose to let go of the pressure to impress and instead receive the peace of knowing we are seen, known, and loved - win or lose.

Petition

Jesus, Prince of Peace,
when pressure rises,
fill my heart with stillness.
Let my thoughts be clear, my body steady,
and my soul anchored in Your love.
You are with me - I will not be shaken.

Closing Prayer

Lord Jesus,
You calmed the storm with a word.
Speak peace into my soul today.
Help me play with clarity, confidence, and calm,
knowing You are by my side in every moment.
Win or lose, let peace be my victory. Amen.

Day 6 – Obedience and Trust in the Coach

Opening Prayers

Hail Mary, full of grace, the Lord is with thee.
Blessed art thou among women, and blessed is the fruit of thy womb, Jesus.
Holy Mary, Mother of God, pray for us sinners, now and at the hour of our death. Amen.

Our Father, who art in heaven, hallowed be Thy name;
Thy kingdom come, Thy will be done on earth as it is in heaven.
Give us this day our daily bread, and forgive us our trespasses,
as we forgive those who trespass against us.
And lead us not into temptation, but deliver us from evil. Amen.

Glory be to the Father, and to the Son, and to the Holy Spirit,
as it was in the beginning, is now, and ever shall be, world without end.
Amen.

Scripture Verse

"Though He was in the form of God… He humbled Himself and became obedient unto death, even death on a cross."
— Philippians 2:6,8

Reflection

A team without obedience falls apart. It doesn't matter how talented the players are, if each one plays for themselves, chaos follows. Unity is built not on individual will, but on a shared trust in leadership. Trusting the coach, even when we don't fully understand the game plan, teaches humility, discipline, and peace. Obedience requires surrendering our pride and learning to listen.

This isn't weakness, it's spiritual strength. Jesus, though equal to the Father in divinity, chose to obey in perfect humility. He followed the will of the Father all the way to the Cross, not because He lacked power, but because He loved perfectly. If Christ embraced obedience even when it cost Him everything, how can we not strive to do the same?

Today, we will honor our coaches, not only with our actions, but with our attitudes. We will listen with respect. We will accept correction without defensiveness. Even if we disagree with decisions made, we will respond with maturity and grace. Obedience shapes the heart. It forms in us a spirit that is open, humble, and willing to be led. And that, more than any skill drill, will prepare us to be both better athletes and better disciples of Christ.

Petition

Jesus, obedient Son of the Father,
help me to listen, even when I disagree.
Let me take correction without defensiveness,
follow instructions with a willing spirit,
and trust that You are shaping me through those in authority.

Closing Prayer

Lord Jesus,
You taught us that true greatness comes through service.
Help me to obey with humility and grace.
Make me a joy to coach,
and an example of trust and discipline.
May Your will be done in me, on the field and in life. Amen.

Day 7 – Gratitude for the Gift of the Game

Opening Prayers

Hail Mary, full of grace, the Lord is with thee.
Blessed art thou among women, and blessed is the fruit of thy womb, Jesus.
Holy Mary, Mother of God, pray for us sinners, now and at the hour of our
death. Amen.

Our Father, who art in heaven, hallowed be Thy name;
Thy kingdom come, Thy will be done on earth as it is in heaven.
Give us this day our daily bread, and forgive us our trespasses,
as we forgive those who trespass against us.
And lead us not into temptation, but deliver us from evil. Amen.

Glory be to the Father, and to the Son, and to the Holy Spirit,
as it was in the beginning, is now, and ever shall be, world without end.
Amen.

Scripture Verse

"Give thanks in all circumstances; for this is the will of God in Christ Jesus
for you."
— 1 Thessalonians 5:18

Reflection

It's easy to take the game for granted. To focus on sore muscles, missed chances, tough losses, or calls that didn't go our way. But underneath every frustration lies a greater truth: the very ability to play, to run, to compete, is a gift. Today, we choose to step back and see the bigger picture - this game is a blessing.

How many people would love to be in our shoes today? To be healthy enough to play, to be surrounded by teammates, to feel the joy of the game pulsing through their veins. Every pass, every challenge, every high and low is part of something bigger. Gratitude lifts our eyes from ourselves to God, from pressure to purpose. It transforms the ordinary moments into sacred ones.

Gratitude turns the field into a sanctuary. It opens our hearts to joy, softens our spirit toward others, and grounds us in the present. And when we thank God before the outcome, before we know whether we will win or lose, we make the game an act of worship. We tell Him, *"This is Yours. And we are Yours."* That kind of gratitude is powerful. It sanctifies not just the match, but our souls.

Petition

Jesus, Giver of all good things,
thank You for the gift of soccer -
for health, ability, friendships, and joy.
Open my eyes to the blessings around me.
Let me never forget that all I have is from You.

Closing Prayer

Lord Jesus Christ,
I praise You not just when I win,
but in every moment of the game.
May my joy on the field reflect Your goodness.
Let gratitude guard my heart from complaint,
and fill me with peace that lasts beyond the final whistle. Amen.

Day 8 – Playing with Purpose

Opening Prayers

Hail Mary, full of grace, the Lord is with thee.
Blessed art thou among women, and blessed is the fruit of thy womb, Jesus.
Holy Mary, Mother of God, pray for us sinners, now and at the hour of our
death. Amen.

Our Father, who art in heaven, hallowed be Thy name;
Thy kingdom come, Thy will be done on earth as it is in heaven.
Give us this day our daily bread, and forgive us our trespasses,
as we forgive those who trespass against us.
And lead us not into temptation, but deliver us from evil. Amen.

Glory be to the Father, and to the Son, and to the Holy Spirit,
as it was in the beginning, is now, and ever shall be, world without end.
Amen.

Scripture Verse

"Whatever you do, in word or deed, do everything in the name of the Lord
Jesus."
— Colossians 3:17

Reflection

This game is not just about running, scoring, or winning. It's not merely about performance or perfection, stats or scouts. Beneath the surface, there is a deeper calling. Every time we lace up our cleats, we carry more than a uniform, we carry a mission. God did not give us these gifts simply for our own glory, but to shape us into the people He created us to be.

The field is a classroom. The game is a teacher. In its discipline, we learn self-mastery. In its competition, we learn courage. In its teamwork, we learn sacrifice. Each moment becomes a choice: Will we play for ourselves, or for something greater? Will we compete with pride, or with love?

When we give our full effort - not out of pride, but out of devotion - our hustle becomes a prayer. Our sportsmanship becomes a witness. Our perseverance becomes a reflection of Christ. We were not made to drift through life, or drift through this game. We were made to live with purpose. Today, we step onto the field not only as athletes, but as disciples. We compete for the Kingdom.

Petition

Jesus, my King and my Goal,
give me clarity of purpose.
Help me compete with meaning,
train with intention,
and never forget why I began.
Let me use this sport as a path to holiness.

Closing Prayer

Lord Jesus Christ,
You lived with perfect purpose, every word, every act, every step.
Help me follow Your example today.
Let me play with joy, passion, and a heart turned toward Heaven.
When others see me, may they glimpse You. Amen.

Day 9 – Offering It All to Christ the King

Opening Prayers

Hail Mary, full of grace, the Lord is with thee.
Blessed art thou among women, and blessed is the fruit of thy womb, Jesus.
Holy Mary, Mother of God, pray for us sinners, now and at the hour of our death. Amen.

Our Father, who art in heaven, hallowed be Thy name;
Thy kingdom come, Thy will be done on earth as it is in heaven.
Give us this day our daily bread, and forgive us our trespasses,
as we forgive those who trespass against us.
And lead us not into temptation, but deliver us from evil. Amen.

Glory be to the Father, and to the Son, and to the Holy Spirit,
as it was in the beginning, is now, and ever shall be, world without end.
Amen.

Scripture Verse

"For from Him and through Him and to Him are all things.
To Him be glory forever. Amen."
— Romans 11:36

Reflection

This novena has been a journey of the heart, one of sacrifice, reflection, and growing closer to the One who reigns above every field, every scoreboard, every trophy. Each prayer has been an invitation to deeper trust, and every day a reminder that this game, like life itself, is not ultimately about us as individuals. It is about Him.

Win or lose, score or stumble, every moment has been offered to Christ. The victories reminded us of His generosity. The defeats taught us humility and trust. Through it all, He was there, not just as a silent observer, but as a living presence on the field of our souls.

The game belongs to Him. Our talents are not self-made, they are gifts, entrusted to us by a loving Creator. Even our desire for greatness is not bad, it was placed in our hearts to be fulfilled not through worldly glory, but through holiness. When that desire is united to Christ's mission and surrendered to His will, it becomes something eternal.

Today, we lay everything at His feet: our effort, our sweat, our goals, our fears, our joy, our pain. We hold nothing back. We give Him the whole journey - not just the highlights, but the struggles too. And we trust that He will take it, sanctify it, and use it to form us into the athletes, teammates, and saints we are called to be. Our King, Our Captain, Our Lord - we offer You everything.

Petition

Jesus, King of Heaven and Earth,
I offer You everything: my past, my present, my future,
my victories and defeats, my joy and my pain.
Take this game, this season, this life,
and use it all for Your Kingdom.

Closing Prayer

Lord Jesus Christ, my Captain and my King,
I give You all that I am.
May this tournament bear fruit in my soul.
May every breath I've taken on the field
be a song of praise to You.
Take my effort, my heart, my love—
and reign in them forever. Amen.

30-Day Offseason Devotional

(or whenever you have need)

Topical Overview

Day	Title / Theme	Focus
1	Silence & Listening	Learning to hear God's voice
2	Morning Offering	Giving the whole day to God
3	Discipline of the Body	Uniting training to spiritual purpose
4	Temptation & Small Victories	Small resistance to temptation
5	Friendship & Fellowship	Trust, support and connection
6	Hard Work in Hiddenness	Effort for the sake of effort
7	Rest and Recovery	Downtime matters
8	Holy Habits	Developing good habits
9	Silence and Stillness	Decompressing and focus
10	Serving Others	Giving back
11	Guarding the eyes	Recognizing goodness, beauty, truth
12	Power of Prayer	Training for the soul
13	The Gift of Time	Make the most of the time we have
14	Honoring Parents & Family	Remembering who supports us
15	Victory over Laziness	Discipline over sloth
16	Offering Pain	Redemptive suffering
17	Joy in Simplicity	Finding delight in the small
18	Speaking Life	Encouraging words, on and off the field
19	The Gift of the Mass	Worship as a spiritual fuel source
20	Confidence in God	Rejecting fear and anxiety
21	Training with Intention	Focused preparation, not distraction
22	Patience in Waiting	Trusting God's timing
23	Brotherhood / Sisterhood	Deep Christian friendship
24	Witness in Public	Being unashamed of Christ
25	Avoiding Laziness	Rejecting the lie of comfort
26	Justice and Fair Play	Doing what's right even when hard
27	Heaven is the Goal	Keeping eternity in mind
28	Sacredness of the Body	Treating your body as God's temple
29	Strength through Mary	Asking for Our Lady's help in virtue
30	Finishing the Race	Persevering to the end for Christ

Day 1 – Silence & Listening

"Be still and know that I am God." – Psalm 46:10

Reflection

In the rush of daily life, and especially in sports, we grow used to movement, noise, and action. The offseason, however, invites us into a different kind of training: silence. True silence is more than just the absence of sound. It is the intentional quieting of our hearts so we can hear the voice of God.

Many saints found their strength not in the noise of the crowd, but in the stillness of prayer. Jesus Himself often withdrew to deserted places to pray. If the Son of God needed silence, how much more do we?

Silence is not easy. It confronts us with ourselves. But in silence, distractions fall away, and the deeper desires of our hearts rise to the surface. In this sacred space, we learn who we really are—and more importantly, who God is.

Today is not about doing more. It is about being still. It is about letting the Lord speak, not through thunder or fire, but in the whisper of peace that only silence brings.

Spiritual Challenge

Spend 10 minutes today in total silence before God. No phone. No music. No distractions. Just you and the Lord. Ask Him to speak—and listen.

Closing Prayer

Lord Jesus, teach me to be still. Calm my restless thoughts and give me the courage to be silent. Speak, Lord—Your servant is listening. Amen.

Day 2 – Morning Offering

"Whatever you do, do everything for the glory of God." – 1 Corinthians 10:31

Reflection

Every day begins with a choice. Will I live for myself, or for God? The morning is a sacred threshold, a moment where we can hand over our time, energy, and intentions to Christ before the day even unfolds.

In the spiritual life, the practice of a 'morning offering' is powerful. It means that before checking your phone, before lacing up your shoes or stepping onto the field, you pause to give everything - success, failure, joy, suffering - to Jesus.

This transforms your whole day into an act of worship. Even ordinary actions, when united with Christ, become holy. For an athlete, this means every sprint, pass, recovery, and rest can be part of your offering to God.

Today, don't wait to find God later. Begin with Him.

Spiritual Challenge

Before doing anything else tomorrow morning, kneel at your bedside or stand in prayer. Offer Jesus your day. Speak from the heart or use a traditional morning offering. Give Him everything—before it begins.

Closing Prayer

Lord Jesus, I offer You this day—my thoughts, my words, my actions, my training, my rest. Let it all glorify You. May I walk in Your will from the first moment to the last. Amen.

Day 3 – Discipline of the Body

"I discipline my body and keep it under control, lest after preaching to others I myself should be disqualified." – 1 Corinthians 9:27

Reflection

In a world that prizes comfort and ease, choosing discipline, especially in the offseason, is an act of spiritual strength. For athletes, discipline isn't just about training; it's about ordering our passions, developing consistency, and becoming good stewards of the gifts we've received. St. Paul reminds us that even our bodies must be brought under the rule of Christ.

The offseason is when champions are made, not by flashy moments, but through quiet, repeated acts of effort and restraint. This discipline, rooted in love, forms not just the athlete, but the whole person.

What we do with our bodies reflects the state of our souls. Every stretch, every rep, every early wake-up is a chance to say, "Lord, this body is Yours. Make it strong for Your glory."

Spiritual Challenge

Choose one area today to be physically disciplined, whether it's waking up on time, finishing a workout, skipping junk food, or going to bed early. Offer that discipline as a prayer for someone in need.

Closing Prayer

Lord Jesus, You fasted, labored, and walked the road of sacrifice. Help me discipline my body not for pride, but for holiness. Strengthen me inside and out, that I may serve You with all that I am. Amen.

Day 4 – Temptation & Small Victories

"No temptation has overtaken you that is not common to man. God is faithful, and he will not let you be tempted beyond your strength."
– 1 Corinthians 10:13

Reflection

Temptation doesn't go away in the offseason, it often increases. With more free time, we're more vulnerable to distractions, laziness, and unhealthy habits. But even the smallest resistance to temptation is a victory.

Jesus was tempted in the desert, and yet He remained faithful. He shows us that temptation is not a sin, but a battleground. Our small "yes" to virtue is a big "no" to the enemy.

Don't underestimate the power of small choices. Turning off a screen, saying a quick prayer, or choosing honesty over ease may seem minor, but these victories build strength, virtue, and holiness.

Spiritual Challenge

Identify one temptation you struggle with during the offseason. Today, name it, pray about it, and resist it. Offer your resistance as a gift to Jesus.

Closing Prayer

Jesus, You faced every temptation and overcame. Help me in my weakness. Give me courage when I'm tempted and remind me that every small victory is a step toward holiness. Amen.

Day 5 – Friendship & Fellowship

"Iron sharpens iron, and one man sharpens another." – Proverbs 27:17

Reflection

The people around us shape us, whether we realize it or not. True friends build us up, call us higher, and walk with us toward God. In the offseason, relationships can either distract us or draw us closer to Christ.

Jesus surrounded Himself with a community, and so should we. Real friendship isn't just about laughs or shared interests, it's about helping each other grow. Who we spend time with will often determine who we become.

Today, reflect on your circle. Who is invested in your success? Who builds you up, or doesn't? Who brings you closer to God? Who might be leading you away? And how can *you* be that iron-sharpening friend to someone else?

Spiritual Challenge

Reach out to a friend today and encourage them in their faith or offer to pray for them. Ask God to bless your friendships and make them holy.

Closing Prayer

Lord Jesus, thank You for the gift of friendship. Help me be a light to those around me. Bring good people into my life who lead me toward You, and teach me to be that friend to others. Amen.

Day 6 – Hard Work in Hiddenness

"Your Father who sees in secret will reward you." – Matthew 6:6

Reflection

In the offseason, there's no crowd, no spotlight - just you, the work, and God. This hidden work matters deeply. The best players train when no one's watching. The best saints grow in silence and faithfulness.

Jesus spent 30 years in Nazareth before His public ministry. Those were years of work, prayer, and quiet growth. God values hiddenness, not because it's flashy, but because it's real.

Don't be discouraged if no one sees your effort right now. God sees. He honors every rep, every prayer, every small act done with love.

Spiritual Challenge

Do one act of love, discipline, or training today that no one else will see. Offer it to God alone.

Closing Prayer

Father, thank You for seeing me even in the quiet. Help me to do good when no one's looking. Teach me to love the hidden work that forms my soul.
Amen.

Day 7 – Rest and Recovery

"Come to me, all who labor and are heavy laden, and I will give you rest." – Matthew 11:28

Reflection

The offseason is a time not just for training but for healing and restoration for both body and soul. In a world that often glorifies hustle and constant motion, rest can feel like weakness. But in God's design, rest is not a concession, it is a command. He built the Sabbath into the rhythm of creation itself. Even Christ, in His earthly ministry, withdrew often to quiet places to pray and be renewed.

True rest is not mere inactivity; it is sacred space. It's a holy invitation to pause, to breathe, and to remember that our worth is not found in what we do, but in who we are, children of God. When we rest well, we regain clarity. We create room to hear God's voice again. We remember that the game, our goals, and even our bodies are temporary, but the soul is eternal.

The offseason gives us a gift: a moment to step back from the rush, to lay down our burdens, and to find rest not just in sleep, but in the Lord. This kind of rest prepares us, not to stay idle but to return stronger, clearer, and more deeply rooted in Him.

Spiritual Challenge

Take a real break today, no screens, no pressure. Spend 30 minutes in silence or prayer, letting God refresh you.

Closing Prayer

Jesus, You rested and prayed in quiet places. Help me find true rest in You today. Heal my heart, my mind, and my body. Amen.

Day 8 – Holy Habits

"He who is faithful in a very little is faithful also in much." – Luke 16:10

Reflection

Habits shape our lives far more than we often realize. It's not just the big moments that define us—it's the daily, repeated choices that form the structure of our character and the direction of our soul. In the offseason, when schedules are more flexible and external demands are fewer, we are given a powerful opportunity: the chance to establish new routines, reset, and rebuild our foundations.

Waking early to pray, choosing nourishing food, setting aside time for spiritual reading or silence, these may seem small, but they are anything but insignificant. These simple acts, done with consistency and love, are the building blocks of holiness. Saints weren't made in crowds or on stages; they were formed in the quiet fidelity of daily life.

The offseason is your training ground—not only for sport, but for sanctity. And the habits you form now, when no one is watching, will become the roots that sustain you when the pressure returns. Choose wisely. Begin small. Let each habit become a step toward becoming the person God created you to be.

Spiritual Challenge

Pick one new habit today - spiritual, physical, or mental -and begin it with prayer and intention.

Closing Prayer

Lord, make me faithful in the small things. Help me build habits that lead to holiness and discipline. Amen.

Day 9 – Silence and Stillness

"Be still, and know that I am God." – Psalm 46:10

Reflection

Noise surrounds us constantly. From phones buzzing to screens flashing, from music blaring to thoughts racing, our world is rarely quiet. We are so used to the noise that silence can feel uncomfortable, even unnatural. But it is precisely in that silence where God most often speaks.

The Lord does not shout to compete with our distractions. He whispers. And only those who choose stillness can truly hear Him. In the quiet of the offseason, we're given a gift: the chance to step away from the clamor and reenter the inner sanctuary of the soul, where God waits patiently.

Silence is not emptiness it is fullness without sound. It's the space where truth becomes clear, where wounds begin to heal, and where the restless heart finds peace. In stillness, we remember who we are: beloved sons and daughters. And more importantly, we remember who God is: faithful, present, loving beyond measure.

Turn off the noise. Lay the phone aside. Step outside or kneel quietly in your room. The world will keep spinning, but for a few sacred minutes, be still. The silence is not empty, it's filled with God.

Spiritual Challenge

Find 10 minutes today to sit in complete silence and let God speak to your heart.

Closing Prayer

Lord, teach me to be still. Help me rest in Your presence and hear Your voice above the noise. Amen.

Day 10 – Serving Others

"The greatest among you shall be your servant." – Matthew 23:11

Reflection

Service builds both love and humility, it draws us out of ourselves and into the heart of Christ. Every time we give our time, our attention, or our effort for someone else, especially when it costs us something, we take a step closer to Jesus. He came not to be served, but to serve. And when we serve others, we walk directly in His footsteps.

In the offseason, we often find more margin in our days. Fewer games. Less structure. More freedom. But that freedom is not just for rest or relaxation, it is also an invitation to give. Service doesn't always look dramatic. It might mean helping a sibling, cleaning without being asked, visiting a lonely relative, or doing small acts of kindness in secret. These hidden sacrifices are not lost. God sees them all.

True service is not about earning praise, it's about loving like Christ. It's about stepping into someone else's need and saying, "I am here with you." That kind of love humbles us, softens our hearts, and deepens our joy.

So ask today, and every day: *Who needs me right now? Where can I be Christ's hands and feet?* Then go and serve with joy.

Spiritual Challenge

Find one way to serve someone today: a sibling, a teammate, a stranger. Do it with joy.

Closing Prayer

Jesus, You came not to be served but to serve. Help me love through action. Show me how to serve with a cheerful heart. Amen.

Day 11 – Guarding the Eyes

"The eye is the lamp of the body." – Matthew 6:22

Reflection

What we watch, scroll, and stare at shapes our hearts, often more than we realize. The eyes are a gateway to the soul, and what we feed them has a quiet but powerful influence. In a digital world full of endless content, the call to purity is more urgent than ever. One video, one post, one movie at a time, we're being formed, either for holiness or for distraction and decay.

The offseason presents a unique opportunity. With fewer commitments and more downtime, we get to choose how we fill the space. It's the perfect time to re-evaluate what we consume, not just avoiding what's harmful, but choosing what's good, beautiful, and true. It means turning off what's toxic. It means walking away from what tempts us toward envy, impurity, or numbness. It also means filling that space with things that lift us up: scripture, lives of the saints, beautiful films or music, and time spent in real, meaningful conversation.

There's an old truth: *Garbage in, garbage out. Holiness in, holiness out.* What we allow into our minds will eventually flow from our hearts into our words, our actions, and even our prayers. Choose wisely. The goal is not just to avoid sin, but to train the eyes to see as Christ sees, and to find joy in the light.

Spiritual Challenge

Go without one form of screen/media today and replace it with Scripture or a spiritual book.

Closing Prayer

Lord, help me guard my eyes. Purify what I see and desire. Make my heart clean and focused on You. Amen.

Day 12 – The Power of Prayer

"Pray without ceasing." – 1 Thessalonians 5:17

Reflection

Prayer is the heartbeat of a Christian life. Just as the heart silently pumps life through the body, prayer quietly sustains the soul. It's not an optional bonus, it's oxygen. And, in the quieter rhythm of offseason life, when the noise of competition fades and the calendar opens up, we are given a sacred opportunity: to go deeper.

Too often we think prayer requires eloquence, a perfect setting, or a special feeling. But it doesn't. What God wants is not polished words, but a present heart. A whispered "Jesus, help me" means more than a hundred distracted recitations. A few minutes of silent surrender can outweigh an hour of mindless routine. What matters is that we show up, that we speak, listen, and offer our hearts again and again.

Use this offseason to reestablish the habit of prayer. Make it the first thing you do when you rise, and the last thing before bed. Take moments during the day to lift your eyes to Heaven. Let your training, rest, meals, and even setbacks be offered in prayer. Over time, prayer becomes your fuel, igniting your passion, healing your wounds, and anchoring your identity in Christ.

The field will one day call again. Let this be the season when your soul was strengthened more than your legs, and your heart learned to beat with His.

Spiritual Challenge

Pray three times today: morning, midday, and night. Keep it simple, but real.

Closing Prayer

Jesus, help me stay close to You through prayer. Let my words rise like incense and draw me deeper into Your heart. Amen.

Day 13 – The Gift of Time

"Teach us to number our days, that we may gain a heart of wisdom." – Psalm 90:12

Reflection

Time is a gift, not a guarantee. Every breath we take, every sunrise we see, every moment we live is a grace given, not something owed. The offseason may feel like a wide stretch of open time, but it moves quickly. One day melts into the next, and before we know it, we're back on the field, back in the rush, back in the noise. What will we have done with the space we were given?

Scripture tells us to "redeem the time," because the days are precious (Ephesians 5:16). Time is not just something to fill, it's something to *invest*. Each day, each hour, is a coin we can spend toward growth, virtue, service, prayer, and love, or toward distraction, laziness, and self-indulgence. The difference isn't usually dramatic, it's subtle. The choice to pray instead of scroll. The choice to train instead of complain. The choice to serve instead of sleep in. Over time, those little choices form the person we become.

The offseason is not a break from becoming holy, rather it's a prime time for it. So, ask yourself honestly: How am I using my time? Am I drawing closer to Christ, or drifting from Him? Am I planting seeds of discipline, prayer, and virtue—or wasting hours?

You don't need to be perfect. You just need to be aware, and willing. God is ready to multiply even your smallest effort when it's given with love.

Spiritual Challenge

Track how you spend your time today. Ask God to help you reclaim any wasted hours.

Closing Prayer

Lord, help me use my time well. Teach me to treasure each hour and fill it with love, effort, and meaning. Amen.

Day 14 – Honoring Parents and Family

"Honor your father and your mother." – Exodus 20:12

Reflection

The offseason often means more time at home: fewer practices, fewer trips, fewer games. While that can feel like a break from the routine of competition, it's a powerful opportunity, a chance to love the people God has placed closest to us.

Family is our first team. Our parents, siblings, and loved ones are not just background characters in our lives, they are part of our calling. Too often, we take them for granted. We assume they'll always be there. We get comfortable, distracted, or impatient. But the truth is, every moment with family is a chance to grow in love and holiness. God sees what we do in secret, especially in how we treat those under our own roof.

This offseason, make a choice to be *intentional* at home. Speak kindly, even when you're tired. Help out, even when it's not your job. Show love in small ways, a hug, a thank-you, a sincere apology. Ask your parents how their day was. Play with your siblings. Write a note. Pray with them. These little acts don't go unnoticed in Heaven.

Loving your family well is one of the most Christlike things you can do. Jesus spent 30 hidden years with Mary and Joseph before His public ministry began. If it was enough for Him, it is holy for us too.

Let home become your training ground for sainthood, one act of love at a time.

Spiritual Challenge

Do one unexpected act of love for your parents or family today.

Closing Prayer

Father God, thank You for my family. Help me love and honor them with my words, actions, and time. Amen.

Day 15 – Victory Over Laziness

"Go to the ant, O sluggard; consider her ways, and be wise." – Proverbs 6:6

Reflection

Laziness is the quiet enemy of greatness. It rarely comes loudly or obviously, it creeps in gently, disguised as "just a break," "just this once," or "I'll get to it later." But left unchecked, it begins to dull the spirit, weaken the will, and waste the gifts God has given us.

God did not create us for mediocrity. He formed us with strength, purpose, and the ability to grow. Every talent - athletic, spiritual, intellectual -is a gift entrusted to us not for comfort, but for mission. When we choose sloth over discipline, distraction over diligence, we're not just hurting our performance, we're turning away from the greatness God made us for.

The offseason is a gift. It's a time of rest, but rest ordered toward renewal, not indulgence. True rest prepares the soul to rise again with vigor. Laziness does the opposite, it makes the soul sluggish, bored, and aimless. This is the time to strengthen the habit of *getting up*. Rise early. Train, even when you don't feel like it. Pray, even when it's dry. Do the small things with excellence. These daily choices will build a strong heart, not just on the field, but for life.

Christ calls us to diligence, not just in sport, but in the soul. He never wasted time. He never quit early. He gave everything. So fight the drift. Shake off the excuses. You were made for more than comfort. You were made for greatness in Him.

Spiritual Challenge

Tackle one task you've been avoiding today. Offer it to God as an act of love.

Closing Prayer

Jesus, help me overcome sloth and procrastination. Fill me with motivation and joy in hard work. Amen.

Day 16 – Offering Pain – Redemptive Suffering

"Now I rejoice in my sufferings for your sake... and in my flesh I am filling up what is lacking in the afflictions of Christ. – Colossians 1:24"

Reflection

Pain is a part of training. Whether it's sore muscles, physical therapy, or emotional discouragement, it comes to every athlete. But Christ transforms pain; He redeems it. When we unite our suffering with His, it becomes a powerful offering of love.

The world teaches us to avoid discomfort at all costs. But the Gospel calls us to carry our crosses with joy. In pain, we meet Christ on His Way to Calvary. In fatigue, we lean on His strength. In disappointment, we draw closer to His pierced heart.

Your aches are not pointless. When offered with love, they can build spiritual strength, purify intention, and even bless others. Today, do not run from the hard moments. Face them, carry them, and lift them up to God. Let your pain have purpose.

Spiritual Challenge

Offer today's hardest moment, physical or emotional, to Christ for someone in need.

Closing Prayer

Jesus, I offer You my aches, my injuries, and my frustrations. Let my pain be united with Yours on the Cross and turned into love. Amen.

Day 17 – Joy in Simplicity – Finding Delight in the Small

"I have learned to be content with whatever I have. – Philippians 4:11"

Reflection

In the offseason, life slows down. Without games or big events, it's easy to feel restless or bored. But Christ invites us to find joy not just in the big wins, but in the quiet, hidden things: a meal with family, a sunset run, a moment of peace in prayer.

The saints teach us that holiness is found in the present moment. When we are always rushing ahead or grasping for the next high, we miss the gift right in front of us. Simplicity isn't boring, it's freeing. It teaches us to love reality, to be present, and to see God in the ordinary.

Choose joy today. Not the loud kind that depends on circumstances, but the quiet kind rooted in gratitude and peace. Let simplicity be your path to Christ.

Spiritual Challenge

Do one simple thing today—slowly and gratefully. Notice God's presence in it.

Closing Prayer

Jesus, teach me the joy of simplicity. Help me to see Your gifts in the little moments and to live this day with peace and delight. Amen.

Day 18 – Speaking Life

"Let no corrupting talk come out of your mouths, but only such as is good for building up." – Ephesians 4:29

Reflection

Words have power. What we say can build up or tear down, give life or cause harm. In the offseason, when the spotlight dims, it's easy to let gossip, sarcasm, or complaining slip into our speech. But Christ calls us to something higher.

Speak life. Encourage teammates. Thank your parents. Honor your coaches. Use your words to plant seeds of hope and courage. Every sentence becomes a choice: will I speak like Christ, or like the world?

In silence, we meet God. In speech, we reveal Him—or obscure Him. Choose today to be a voice of blessing, even when no one else is. Your words matter. Let them echo heaven.

Spiritual Challenge

Give a sincere word of encouragement to someone today.

Closing Prayer

Jesus, purify my lips. Let my words bless, not wound. Teach me to speak with love, truth, and grace. Amen.

Day 19 – The Gift of the Mass

"Do this in remembrance of Me." – Luke 22:19

Reflection

The Holy Mass is the highest form of worship on earth—heaven meeting earth in mystery and power. In it, Christ offers Himself anew, and we are invited to receive Him body, blood, soul, and divinity. There is nothing more sacred, more strengthening, or more life-giving.

In the offseason, our schedule often becomes looser. This is a blessing in disguise. It allows us more time to attend daily or weekly Mass with intention -not just out of obligation, but as a personal offering of love.

Mass isn't just a ritual; it's a spiritual fuel source. It reminds us of who we are: sons and daughters of God, united in one Body through Christ. It renews our purpose. It fortifies our soul. It forms us into saints.

When we go to Mass, we step out of our own plans and into God's plan. We lay down our distractions and step into communion. We leave changed, little by little, more like Christ.

Spiritual Challenge

Attend a weekday Mass this week. Offer it for someone who has helped you in your soccer journey - spiritually, emotionally, or physically.

Closing Prayer

Lord Jesus, thank You for the gift of the Eucharist. Help me never to take it for granted. Draw me into the mystery of Your love at every Mass, and shape me into the athlete, disciple, and person You created me to be. Amen.

Day 20 – Confidence in God

"The Lord is my light and my salvation; whom shall I fear?" –
Psalm 27:1

Reflection

Fear and doubt creep in when we put our confidence in things
that fade like talent, approval, and success. But when our trust is
in the Lord, we stand on unshakable ground.

Offseason is the perfect time to deepen that trust. When the
pressure lifts and the noise quiets down, we can ask: Where is my
confidence rooted? Is it in Christ or in myself?

Confidence in God is not arrogance, it's peace. It's walking into
the unknown without fear because you know Who goes with you.
Let your offseason be filled with holy courage, born not from ego
but from the security of being God's beloved child.

Spiritual Challenge

Pray the Psalm: 'The Lord is my shepherd… I shall not want.' Let
it become your anthem of trust.

Closing Prayer

*Jesus, I place my trust in You. Take away my fear and fill me with courage.
Amen.*

Day 21 – Training with Intention

"Every athlete exercises self-control in all things. They do it to receive a perishable wreath, but we wear an imperishable one."
— 1 Corinthians 9:25

Reflection

It's easy to go through the motions: show up, stretch, get your reps in, and call it a day. But greatness, spiritual or athletic, never grows out of being on autopilot. It grows from focus. From purpose. From *intention*.

God gave you a body and a mind. Your offseason training isn't just about staying fit, it's a chance to grow in virtue: discipline, perseverance, clarity, and commitment. When you train with Christ in mind, your workouts become more than preparation, they become worship.

Every lift, every run, every drill can become an offering. What matters is how you show up: are you present? Focused? Aware of your goals? Aware of *why* you're doing it?

Training with intention means every action has meaning. And when your body is formed with purpose, your soul follows suit. God doesn't just want your hustle, He wants your *heart* behind it.

Spiritual Challenge

Write down your physical and spiritual goals for this week. Before each training session, pause and offer it to God.

Closing Prayer

Lord Jesus, help me to train with purpose. Let every movement, every rep, and every breath be offered to You. Form in me a spirit of focus and love, not just for sport, but for the Kingdom. Amen.

Day 22 – Patience in Waiting

"Wait for the Lord; be strong, and let your heart take courage;
wait for the Lord!"
— Psalm 27:14

Reflection

The offseason can feel slow. Progress isn't always visible. The
next season feels far off. But waiting is not wasted time, used with
purpose it becomes holy time. Scripture is full of people who
waited: Abraham for a child, Moses for the Promised Land, Mary
for the fullness of God's plan. In every case, waiting became the
place where God did His deepest work.

Patience is not passive. It's an active trust in God's timing, a
discipline of the heart. It means believing that He's forming you
in the silence, in the hidden work, in the moments when nothing
seems to be happening.

When we rush, we miss what God is doing beneath the surface.
Like seeds in soil, our growth often starts unseen. The offseason
is your soil. Be still. Be faithful. Show up day after day. Trust that
God sees you, hears you, and is preparing you.

Spiritual Challenge

Spend 10 minutes in silent prayer today. Don't speak. Just listen.
Surrender your timetable to God.

Closing Prayer

*Lord, You are never late. Teach me to wait with peace and trust. Shape me in
the quiet, stretch my patience, and deepen my faith. I believe that You are
working, even when I cannot see. Amen.*

Day 23 – Brotherhood / Sisterhood

"Behold, how good and pleasant it is when brothers dwell in unity!"
— Psalm 133:1

Reflection

God never meant for us to walk this journey alone. We were made for community, for real friendships rooted not just in laughter or shared interests, but in Christ. Whether it's your teammates, siblings, or a small circle of trusted friends, true brotherhood and sisterhood push you toward holiness.

On the field, you win and lose together. In faith, you grow stronger together. A good teammate doesn't just pass the ball; they lift you up when you fall. A good brother or sister in Christ speaks the truth in love, challenges you to be better, and stays by your side when life gets messy.

In the offseason, you have time to deepen these friendships. Invest in them. Pray together. Share your struggles. Cheer each other on in virtue and in training. Brotherhood and sisterhood built on Christ will carry you through more than just a game, they'll carry you toward Heaven.

Spiritual Challenge

Reach out to a friend today and ask how you can pray for them. If possible, pray together, even just a short prayer over the phone.

Closing Prayer

Jesus, You called the disciples not just to follow You, but to walk together. Teach me how to be a true brother or sister in faith. Help me build others up, speak with kindness, and love as You love. Amen.

Day 24 – Witness in Public

"You are the light of the world. A city set on a hill cannot be hidden."
— Matthew 5:14

Reflection

It's easy to talk about Jesus in church or at home. But what about on the field? At school? Online? In the real world, when eyes are watching and the pressure is real, will we stand for Him?

Witnessing doesn't mean preaching on a street corner. It means living so differently, so joyfully, so faithfully, that others can't help but notice. It's how you treat your teammates, how you respond to unfair calls, how you handle wins and losses, how you speak when no coach is around.

You don't have to wear a giant cross to witness. Just be kind when others are cruel. Be patient when others snap. Pray before a game. Speak up for what's right. These small actions shine bright.

The offseason is a time to strengthen your courage, to get comfortable living your faith out loud. The world doesn't need more noise. It needs more light.

Spiritual Challenge

Do something public today that shows your faith, a prayer before a meal, a mention of God in conversation, a post that honors Christ.

Closing Prayer

Jesus, You are my light and my salvation. Give me courage to live my faith openly and humbly. Let others see You in me—not for my glory, but for Yours. Amen.

Day 25 – Avoiding Laziness

"Whatever your hand finds to do, do it with all your might."
— Ecclesiastes 9:10

Reflection

Laziness rarely shows up as full rebellion—it comes quietly. One skipped workout. One late morning. One "I'll do it tomorrow." Before long, excellence is replaced by excuses.

But God didn't make us for mediocrity. He made us to be fully alive, to train, to love, to pray, to grow. Laziness steals that. It dulls the edge of our soul and weakens our desire for greatness. And it doesn't just affect our bodies - it seeps into our spiritual life too.

In the offseason, the temptation to slack off is strong. But this is when champions are built. This is when saints grow in secret. Choose diligence. Not out of guilt, but out of love for God who gave you every breath, every ability, every opportunity.

Holiness requires effort. So does greatness in any area of life. Reject the lie that comfort is your friend. Christ never chose the easy path, He chose the Cross. And so will we.

Spiritual Challenge

Identify one area where you've been lazy - spiritual, physical, or mental. Make a plan today to change that pattern.

Closing Prayer

Jesus, stir up in me a spirit of discipline and joy in hard work. Help me to rise each day with purpose and to reject every temptation to settle. I want to give You my best, not my leftovers. Amen.

Day 26 – Justice and Fair Play

"Learn to do good; seek justice, correct oppression; bring justice to the fatherless, plead the widow's cause."
— Isaiah 1:17

Reflection

In sport, as in life, we're often tempted to bend the rules, to foul when no one sees, to cheat just a little, to take what hasn't been earned. But justice matters to God. He is a God of truth, of fairness, of righteousness. He sees the hidden moments. He honors the choices that reflect His heart.

Fair play isn't weakness. It's strength under control. It's the quiet decision to walk in the light when others hide in the dark. And justice doesn't end on the field, it extends to how we treat others off it: the kid who gets picked last, the one who gets mocked, the teammate who's struggling.

The offseason is a chance to build integrity. Are you fair when there's no ref? Are you honest when no one's watching? Do you protect the weak, or ignore them? These are the moments that form a just heart, one that reflects the justice and mercy of Christ.

Spiritual Challenge

Make one decision today that defends someone who is overlooked or mistreated, even if it costs you something.

Closing Prayer

Jesus, You are the Just Judge and the Merciful Savior. Teach me to walk in fairness, to do what is right even when it's hard, and to stand up for those who cannot stand for themselves. Amen.

Day 27 – Heaven is the Goal

"But our citizenship is in heaven, and from it we await a Savior, the Lord Jesus Christ."
— Philippians 3:20

Reflection

Trophies fade. Stats are forgotten. But Heaven lasts forever.

It's easy to get caught up in success: who starts, who scores, who wins the medal. But God calls us to lift our eyes higher. Earthly rewards are good, but they are not the goal. The real prize is eternity with Christ.

The saints understood this. They played, prayed, worked, and suffered, all with their eyes fixed on Heaven. Every day was a step toward the finish line of eternal life. And we're invited to run that same race.

What does this mean in the offseason? It means training for more than a season—it means training for sainthood. It means letting your choices, your relationships, and your quiet moments be shaped by the reality that Heaven is your home.

Live like a child of the Kingdom. Compete with joy. Love sacrificially. And never forget: the game ends. Heaven doesn't.

Spiritual Challenge

Take five quiet minutes today to reflect on eternity. Ask God to renew your desire for Heaven, and the grace to live like it's your destination.

Closing Prayer

Lord Jesus, remind me that this world is not my home. Keep my eyes on Heaven, my heart rooted in You, and my life aimed at eternal glory. Help me to play, train, and live for the crown that never fades. Amen.

Day 28 – Sacredness of the Body

"Do you not know that your body is a temple of the Holy Spirit within you, whom you have from God?"
— 1 Corinthians 6:19

Reflection

In the world of sports, the body is often treated as a tool, or even an idol. Athletes are told to sculpt it, push it, dominate with it. But Scripture tells a deeper truth: your body is holy. It's not just a machine. It's a temple.

God created your body. He designed it with purpose. He filled it with breath and strength and movement. And through baptism, He made it a dwelling place of the Holy Spirit. That means how you treat your body matters, not just for performance, but for your soul.

Do you honor your body with what you eat, how you rest, what you watch? Do you avoid things that damage it, misuse it, or ignore its needs? Holiness includes the physical. Jesus had a body. He fasted, walked, wept, healed, and ultimately gave His body on the Cross.

In the offseason, you have a chance to care for your body in a sacred way. Not just for strength, but for stewardship. Not just for fitness, but for faith.

Spiritual Challenge

Choose one way today to honor your body as a temple—through food, sleep, purity, or care—and offer it to God in gratitude.

Closing Prayer

Holy Spirit, You dwell within me. Teach me to see my body as sacred, not selfish. Help me to treat it with respect, discipline, and gratitude, so that it may glorify You in all things. Amen.

Day 29 – Strength through Mary

"Behold, I am the handmaid of the Lord; let it be to me according to your word."
— Luke 1:38

Reflection

Mary was not an athlete. She never ran a race or took the field. But she is the strongest woman the world has ever known.

Her strength wasn't in muscle or might, it was in surrender. She said "yes" to God with her whole being, even when it cost her everything. In her quiet obedience, in her hidden sacrifices, in her unwavering love for Jesus, she showed the kind of strength that transforms the world.

We need that kind of strength, especially in the hidden training grounds of the offseason. When no one is watching. When the goals feel distant. When spiritual dryness sets in. Mary walks with us there, offering her prayers and example.

She is not just the Mother of God, she's our mother too. She knows what it means to wait, to endure, to suffer with purpose. And she stands ready to help you grow in virtue, if you ask.

When we train with Mary, we don't train alone. We are drawn into her steadiness, her purity, her courage. And she always leads us to her Son.

Spiritual Challenge

Pray a Hail Mary slowly and intentionally today, asking Mary to help you grow in inner strength and spiritual endurance.

Closing Prayer

Mary, gentle and strong, be my mother and my guide. Teach me how to say "yes" to God in every area of life. Walk with me in the quiet moments, the hard workouts, and the hidden sacrifices. Lead me always to Jesus. Amen.

Day 30 – Finishing the Race

"I have fought the good fight, I have finished the race, I have kept the faith."
— 2 Timothy 4:7

Reflection

The end of a race is often the hardest part. Muscles burn. Breathing shortens. Distractions rise. But the finish line calls.

In our faith and in life, finishing matters. Christ didn't stop short, He carried His Cross all the way to Calvary. And He calls us to the same perseverance. Not just in seasons of training or moments of inspiration, but all the way to the end.

The offseason may be closing soon, but the habits, prayers, and growth don't end here. You've built something. You've chosen to train the soul as well as the body. Now is the time to carry it forward into the season—and beyond.

God isn't just forming you into a better athlete. He's forming you into a saint. And saints don't give up. They finish strong, no matter the cost, because they know the prize: not a trophy, but Heaven.

Stay the course. Keep the faith. Run with endurance, eyes on Christ.

Spiritual Challenge

Look back and thank God for what He's taught you this month. Then write down one habit you'll carry with you into the next season.

Closing Prayer

Jesus, You are my finish line. Help me to persevere through every challenge, stay faithful through every season, and live for Your glory in all things. Thank You for walking with me. I offer You my whole life. Amen.

A Daily/Weekly Soccer Rosary

Why This Rosary for Soccer Players?

Soccer is more than a game, it's a school of the soul.

On the field, we learn about discipline, teamwork, sacrifice, and courage. We face moments of triumph and defeat, joy and frustration, unity and loneliness. In many ways, soccer mirrors the Christian life. It asks for our whole heart, demands perseverance, and calls us to love even when it's hard.

The Rosary is one of the greatest spiritual weapons and treasures in the Catholic tradition. When we pray it, we walk with Mary through the life of her Son, Jesus. We meditate not just on events of the past, but on eternal truths that shape how we live, play, and love today.

This Soccer Rosary is a bridge between the pitch and the prayer. It's a way for athletes to bring Christ into their training, competition, and daily life, decade by decade, step by step.

Each mystery reflects on a moment in Christ's life, and invites players to draw strength, humility, and grace from it. Whether before a match, after training, or during travel, this Rosary invites you to unite the beautiful game with the even more beautiful Gospel.

Mary is not just the Mother of Jesus, she is our teammate in the spiritual life. She knows the cost of sacrifice and the glory of victory in God. Invite her to walk with you, pray with you, and help you become the player and person God created you to be.

This is how we followers of Christ play the game... not just for victory on earth, but for glory in Heaven.

How to Pray the Rosary
(instructions)

The Rosary is a meditative prayer that leads us through key moments in the life of Jesus Christ and His Blessed Mother. It uses simple prayers and a set structure to draw our hearts into deeper reflection and union with God.

The Rosary Structure
A standard five-decade Rosary consists of:
- 1 Crucifix – to begin with the Sign of the Cross and the Apostles' Creed
- 1 large bead – for the Our Father
- 3 small beads – for three Hail Marys (for Faith, Hope, and Charity)
- 1 large bead – for the Glory Be and to announce the first Mystery
- 5 sets (decades) of 1 large bead and 10 small beads, each representing one Mystery (Joyful, Luminous, Sorrowful, or Glorious)

Step-by-Step Guide *(common prayers at end of section)*
1. Make the Sign of the Cross -In the Name of the Father, and of the Son, and of the Holy Spirit. Amen.
2. Pray the Apostles' Creed.
3. On the first large bead, pray the Our Father.
4. On the next three small beads, pray three Hail Marys
5. Pray the Glory Be.
6. Announce the First Mystery (e.g., The Annunciation), then pray: Our Father; 10 Hail Marys; Glory Be; Fatima
7. Repeat step 6 for the remaining four Mysteries (total of five).
8. After completing all five decades, pray the: Hail Holy Queen; Concluding Prayer (optional), Finish with the Sign of the Cross

Optional Closing Prayers
- Prayer to St. Michael the Archangel
- Personal intentions or thanksgivings

The Joyful Mysteries
(Traditionally prayed on Mondays and Saturdays)

1. The Annunciation – Luke 1:26–38
"Mary says yes to God's plan."

Soccer Reflection
Every season begins with a "yes." A yes to show up. A yes to work hard. A yes to grow. Mary's fiat wasn't easy, but it was faithful. In soccer, there are moments when we're asked to trust: to take a new role, to accept the bench, to lead when it's hard. Mary teaches us how to respond: not with fear, but with surrender.

Intention
Mary, help me to say yes to God's plan for me, on the field and in life, even when it's uncomfortable.

---

2. The Visitation – Luke 1:39–56
"Mary serves her cousin Elizabeth with joy."

Soccer Reflection
The best players serve their team - not for applause, but out of love. Mary traveled miles to help someone else. On the field, great players lift others up. They pass when others are open. They celebrate their teammates' success. In a world focused on self, Mary shows us how to be other-focused.

Intention
Mary, teach me to be unselfish in my play and generous in spirit. Help me to be a servant on and off the field.

---

3. The Nativity – Luke 2:1–20
"Jesus is born in poverty and simplicity."

Soccer Reflection
Jesus came into the world not with fanfare, but in a humble stable. In soccer, greatness isn't about flash, it's about heart. Some

of the best players are quiet leaders. Some of the most powerful moments come in ordinary settings. Christ teaches us to value humility over hype.

Intention
Mary, help me to play with humility. Remind me that greatness is born in hidden places, through quiet faithfulness.

---

4. The Presentation in the Temple – Luke 2:22–38
"Jesus is offered to God in obedience."

Soccer Reflection
Obedience and sacrifice go hand-in-hand. When Jesus was presented at the temple, He was placed entirely in the Father's hands. Athletes do this when they offer their effort, success, and struggle to God. When we play not just for ourselves but for Him, the game becomes an offering.

Intention
Mary, help me offer every game, every practice, and every moment to God. Let my life be a gift back to Him.

---

5. The Finding of Jesus in the Temple – Luke 2:41–50
"Jesus is found teaching in His Father's house."

Soccer Reflection
Sometimes in sport, we feel lost, doubt, frustration, setbacks. Mary and Joseph searched anxiously for Jesus, only to find Him in the house of His Father. When you feel lost in your sport, seek Him first. In the "temple" of your heart, Jesus is always waiting. Faith and sport must go hand-in-hand if you want true peace.

Intention
Mary, when I feel lost or discouraged, lead me back to Jesus. Help me find Him in prayer, in the Eucharist, and even in the game I love.

The Luminous Mysteries
(Traditionally prayed on Thursdays)

1. The Baptism of Jesus in the Jordan – Matthew 3:13–17
"Jesus is baptized and begins His public ministry."

Soccer Reflection
Every season has a beginning, and baptism is our beginning in Christ. At His baptism, Jesus was affirmed by the Father and anointed by the Spirit. Before any goal or glory, He was claimed by love. As players, our identity must be rooted not in performance, but in the truth: we are beloved children of God. Every time we step on the field, we remember who we are and whose we are.

Intention
Jesus, remind me that my worth comes from being Your beloved child, not from how well I perform.

---

1. The Wedding at Cana – John 2:1–11
"Jesus performs His first miracle at Mary's request."

Soccer Reflection
Jesus turned water into wine, but only after Mary interceded and the servants obeyed. In the game, success comes when we listen, trust, and give our best, even when we don't fully understand. Sometimes we feel like we don't have enough. But Christ takes our "not enough" and makes it more than enough. Offer Him what you have, and let Him do the rest.

Intention
Jesus, when I feel like I don't have enough - strength, skill, courage - transform what I offer You.

3. The Proclamation of the Kingdom – Mark 1:14–15
Jesus preaches repentance and calls us to the Kingdom of God.
Soccer Reflection
Every game has rules. Every team has a goal. Jesus came to announce the Kingdom of God and a way of life with new priorities: repentance, humility, and love. On the field and off, we're called to live by Kingdom values. It's not just about winning games, but bringing light to the world through our play, our attitude, and our witness.

Intention
Jesus, help me live and play in a way that reflects Your Kingdom. Let others see You in me.

---

4. The Transfiguration – Luke 9:28–36
Jesus is transfigured in glory before Peter, James, and John.

Soccer Reflection
The disciples saw Jesus radiant on the mountain, reminding them who He truly was. In soccer, there are moments that reflect glory—victory, perfect passes, team unity. But those moments point to something deeper. Christ reveals our highest calling: to be transformed into saints. Training the body is good, but training the soul for glory is eternal.

Intention
Jesus, transfigure my heart. Let me seek not just excellence in sport, but holiness in life.

---

5. The Institution of the Eucharist – Luke 22:14–20
"Jesus gives us His Body and Blood at the Last Supper."

Soccer Reflection
The Eucharist is the source and summit of our faith. In it, Jesus gives Himself fully. As athletes, we often give our energy and effort to the game, but are we giving our hearts to Christ? Just as

we need fuel for our bodies, we need spiritual nourishment. Mass is the best preparation for life, including sport. From the altar flows strength for every field.

Intention
Jesus, help me hunger for You in the Eucharist. Let Your presence be my strength in every game and trial.

The Sorrowful Mysteries
(Traditionally prayed on Tuesdays and Fridays)

1. The Agony in the Garden – Luke 22:39–46
"Jesus prays in the Garden of Gethsemane, burdened by the suffering to come."

Soccer Reflection
Before big games or moments of uncertainty, we all face anxiety. Jesus knew fear - but He faced it in prayer. Athletes can experience stress: fear of failure, fear of injury, fear of letting others down. In those moments, Jesus teaches us not to hide, but to kneel. The battle begins in the heart. Your courage comes not from suppressing fear, but surrendering it to God.

Intention
Jesus, help me turn to You in times of anxiety. In every high-pressure moment, teach me to pray with trust, not panic.

---

2. The Scourging at the Pillar – John 19:1
"Jesus is whipped and beaten for our sins."

Soccer Reflection
Physical pain is part of the game. Bruises, soreness, fatigue, they come with the territory. Jesus endured suffering with love and without complaint. As athletes, we can unite our physical sacrifices to His. Offering up the soreness, the sprints, and the struggle can turn sport into sanctification. Your body, given in love, becomes a prayer.

Intention
Jesus, help me endure pain with patience. When I train or compete through difficulty, let it be united to Your suffering.

---

3. The Crowning with Thorns – Matthew 27:27–31

"Jesus is mocked and crowned with thorns."

Soccer Reflection
Sometimes athletes face ridicule, disrespect, or false judgment. Jesus endured humiliation silently. He didn't respond with anger, but with dignity. When you're misunderstood or mocked, remember Him. True greatness doesn't come from revenge, but from love under pressure.

Intention
Jesus, give me strength to respond to criticism with grace. Help me to play and live with dignity, even when I'm wronged.

---

4. The Carrying of the Cross – Luke 23:26–31
"Jesus carries His Cross toward Calvary."

Soccer Reflection
The journey is long. Tournaments wear you down. Seasons stretch your stamina. Like Jesus, we all carry crosses. Some are physical, some emotional. But we are not alone. Jesus fell, but He got up. He shows us how to carry the weight, step by step, one faithful stride at a time. And like Simon who helped Him, we too need to carry each other.

Intention
Jesus, help me carry my burdens with faith. Give me strength when I'm weak and courage to help others with theirs.

---

5. The Crucifixion – Luke 23:33–46
"Jesus dies on the Cross for our salvation."

Soccer Reflection
This is the ultimate sacrifice. Christ held nothing back. In soccer and in life, we are called to give everything. Not just in effort, but in love. Jesus' death transforms defeat into victory. So when things don't go our way, we remember: success isn't always measured by the scoreboard, but by how much we loved and offered.

Intention

Jesus, teach me to play and live with total love. Help me give everything for You—no excuses, no holding back.

The Glorious Mysteries of the Rosary
(Traditionally prayed on Wednesdays and Sundays)

1. The Resurrection – Luke 24:1–12
"Jesus rises from the dead."

Soccer Reflection
Victory over death. That's what Christ accomplished. And every victory on the field, small or great ,can remind us of this greater triumph. When we come back from a loss, rise after a fall, or step into a new season, we echo the rhythm of resurrection. Hope is never lost. Christ has won.

Intention
Lord Jesus, may every win remind me of Your victory, and every loss draw me to trust in Your power to raise me up.

---

2. The Ascension – Acts 1:6–11
"Jesus returns to the Father."

Soccer Reflection
Jesus didn't just rise—He ascended, returning to the Father and entrusting His mission to us. In soccer, every training session and every match is a moment of formation. But the goal isn't to stay where we are—it's to grow, to be sent, to elevate our game and our faith. Ascension means rising higher—with purpose.

Intention
Jesus, help me to play with my eyes on Heaven. Let each step I take be a step toward holiness and deeper mission.

---

3. The Descent of the Holy Spirit – Acts 2:1–4
"The Holy Spirit fills the Apostles with courage."

Soccer Reflection

The Spirit empowers. On the field, we need more than strength, we need courage, wisdom, and unity. The Holy Spirit brings fire and clarity. A great team plays with one heart. A great soul lives by the Spirit. Before every match, call on Him. He'll show up.

Intention

Holy Spirit, fill me with boldness. Guide my words, decisions, and movements on and off the field. Make me a joyful witness.

---

4. The Assumption of Mary – Revelation 12:1; Tradition
"Mary is taken body and soul into Heaven."

Soccer Reflection

Mary's life was one long "yes." Her reward? Union with God in glory. She teaches us to give everything in love - to play every game, live every day, as an offering to God. One day, if we follow her path, we too will be welcomed home.

Intention

Mary, assumed into Heaven, help me to live with Heaven in mind. Let my game and my life be full of faith, hope, and love.

---

5. The Coronation of Mary – Revelation 12:1; Tradition
"Mary is crowned Queen of Heaven and Earth."

Soccer Reflection

Mary is crowned not because she dominated, but because she loved fully. In soccer, as in life, the true crown is not for the flashy but for the faithful. Do I seek applause, or do I seek to please God? Mary's crown reminds us: humility wins in Heaven.

Intention

Queen of Heaven, teach me to live with quiet strength and humble love. Crown my efforts with grace, not pride.

Common Rosary Prayers

The Apostles' Creed

I believe in God, the Father Almighty, Creator of heaven and earth, and in Jesus Christ, His only Son, our Lord, who was conceived by the Holy Spirit, born of the Virgin Mary, suffered under Pontius Pilate, was crucified, died and was buried; He descended into hell; on the third day He rose again from the dead; He ascended into heaven, and is seated at the right hand of God the Father Almighty; from there He will come to judge the living and the dead. I believe in the Holy Spirit, the holy Catholic Church, the communion of saints, the forgiveness of sins, the resurrection of the body, and life everlasting. Amen.

Our Father

Our Father, who art in heaven, hallowed be Thy name; Thy kingdom come; Thy will be done on earth as it is in heaven. Give us this day our daily bread; and forgive us our trespasses as we forgive those who trespass against us; and lead us not into temptation, but deliver us from evil. Amen.

Hail Mary

Hail Mary, full of grace, the Lord is with thee; blessed art thou among women, and blessed is the fruit of thy womb, Jesus. Holy Mary, Mother of God, pray for us sinners, now and at the hour of our death. Amen.

Glory Be

Glory be to the Father, and to the Son, and to the Holy Spirit, as it was in the beginning, is now, and ever shall be, world without end. Amen.

Fatima Prayer

O my Jesus, forgive us our sins, save us from the fires of hell, lead all souls to Heaven, especially those in most need of Thy mercy.

Hail, Holy Queen

Hail, Holy Queen, Mother of Mercy, our life, our sweetness and our hope. To thee do we cry, poor banished children of Eve. To thee do we send up our sighs, mourning and weeping in this valley of tears. Turn then, most gracious advocate, thine eyes of mercy toward us, and after this our exile show unto us the blessed fruit of thy womb, Jesus. O clement, O loving, O sweet Virgin Mary. Amen.

Prayer to St. Michael the Archangel

St. Michael the Archangel,
defend us in battle.
Be our protection against the wickedness and snares of the devil.
May God rebuke him, we humbly pray,
and do thou, O Prince of the Heavenly Host,
by the power of God,
cast into hell Satan and all the evil spirits
who prowl about the world seeking the ruin of souls. Amen.

Prayer for Personal Intentions or Thanksgivings

Lord Jesus Christ,
I offer You the intentions of my heart at this moment.
For my team, my family, my coaches, and all those I love—
grant strength, healing, wisdom, and grace.

Thank You for the gift of this game, for the lessons it teaches,
for the joy it brings, and for the way it draws me closer to You.

Help me to glorify You in everything,
whether in victory or in defeat,
in rest or in training,
in silence or in the roar of the crowd.

I place all my prayers, needs, and hopes into Your Sacred Heart.
Jesus, I trust in You. Amen.

Bibliography & Inspirations

This devotional was written to support Catholic athletes, coaches, and families in uniting their love for the beautiful game with their Catholic faith. While most of the reflections, prayers, and meditations are original compositions, they are deeply rooted in the Church's living tradition and drawn from the following sources of inspiration:

- *Sacred Scripture* - Particularly passages from the Revised Standard Version (RSV) and the New American Bible (NAB), used in meditative and devotional form.

- *Traditional Catholic Prayers* - Including the Our Father, Hail Mary, Glory Be, Apostles' Creed, Hail Holy Queen, and the Fatima Prayer.

- *The Catechism of the Catholic Church* - For foundational truths on prayer, virtue, and the Christian life.

- *Spiritual Legacy of the Saints* — Especially the witness of:
    - St. Sebastian, patron saint of athletes
    - St. John Paul II, who saw sports as a path to Holiness
    - St. Joseph, model of strength, humility, and fatherhood
    - Our Lady, Queen of Heaven and our spiritual teammate

- *Personal Experience* — Nearly 50 years of playing, coaching, parenting, and praying through the game of soccer, lived in the domestic church and the community of Catholic sport.

This booklet is offered in a spirit of encouragement and faith. May it serve to draw hearts closer to Christ, through Mary, through sport, and through the daily joys and sacrifices of Catholic life.

www.ingramcontent.com/pod-product-compliance
Lightning Source LLC
Chambersburg PA
CBHW032045040426
42449CB00007B/992